DANCE

HiP-HoP Dancing

by Joan Freese

Consultant:
AleKsa "LeX" Chmiel, Co-Director/Owner
Flomotion Dance Company
Philadelphia, Pennsylvania

Capstone
press
Mankato, Minnesota

Snap Books are published by Capstone Press,
151 Good Counsel Drive, P.O. Box 669, Mankato, Minnesota 56002.
www.capstonepress.com

Library of Congress Cataloging-in-Publication Data

Freese, Joan
    Hip-hop dancing / Joan Freese.
    p. cm.—(Snap books. Dance)
    Summary: "Describes hip-hop dancing, including history, training,
moves, and competition"—Provided by publisher.
    Includes bibliographical references and index.
    ISBN-13: 978-1-4296-0121-4 (hardcover)
    ISBN-10: 1-4296-0121-3 (hardcover)
    1. Hip-hop dance—Juvenile literature. I. Title. II. Series.
GV1796.H57F74 2008
793.3—dc22   2006102783

Editor: Becky Viaene

Designer: Veronica Bianchini

Photo Researchers: Charlene Deyle and Wanda Winch

Photo Credits:
AP Photo/Francois Mori, 26, 27; Capstone Press/Karon Dubke, all except pages 5, 7, 26, 27, 28–29, and 32; Corbis/
Atsuko Tanaka, 5; Courtesy of the author Joan Freese, 32; PhotoEdit Inc./A. Ramey, 28–29; SuperStock, Inc./Prisma, 7

Acknowledgements:
**Joan Freese would like to thank Amy Sackett (b-girl, hip-hop educator, and most generous
collaborator) for her contributions to this book. Thanks also to the other members of
Minneapolis' hip-hop dance company Collective including Arturo Miles, Nikki Cullinen, and
Lisa Berman, for their knowledge and assistance.**

Capstone Press would like to thank Amy Sackett, Lisa Berman (B-girl MonaLisa), Charles Thorstad (B-boy StepChild),
the students of Collective, and Dance Endeavors Studio, in Bloomington, Minnesota, for their assistance with this book.

Table of Contents

Chapter One

BACK TO THE OLD SCHOOL

HIP-HOP DANCE IS ABOUT MORE THAN JUST SHOWING OFF YOUR MOVES—IT'S A LIFESTYLE.

Hip-hop's rich roots date back to the "old school." This respectful term simply means how hip-hop was once done.

Hip-hop was born in the Bronx, in New York City, in the 1970s and 1980s. At parks and dance clubs, kids invented today's hip-hop culture. DJs spun records. MCs rapped clever rhymes about their lives. Artists sprayed colorful graffiti on buildings. And hip-hop dancers used amazing energy to create an exciting new dance form.

Chapter Two

IT'S A HIP-HOP WORLD

TODAY, HIP-HOP DANCE IS EVERYWHERE.

You see hip-hop dancing in music videos, commercials, and cartoons. And hip-hop has gone international. You could say it's a hip-hop world!

Across the globe, dancers base new moves off the original hip-hop dance styles of popping, locking, toprocking, and breaking. But dancers don't use just these styles, because hip-hop moves continue to expand.

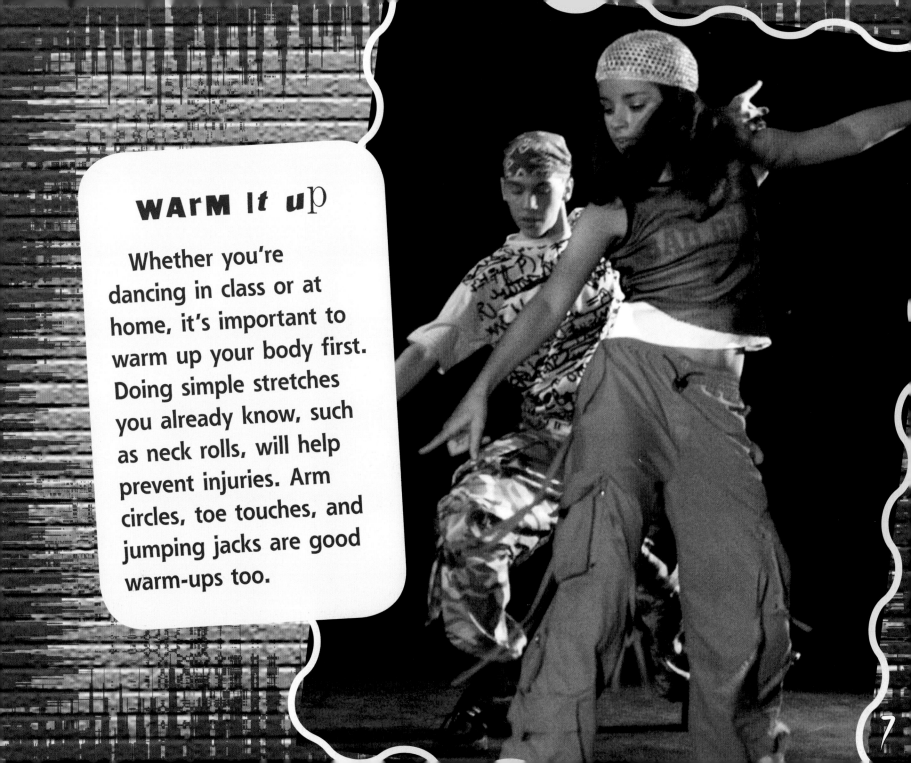

WArM It uP

Whether you're dancing in class or at home, it's important to warm up your body first. Doing simple stretches you already know, such as neck rolls, will help prevent injuries. Arm circles, toe touches, and jumping jacks are good warm-ups too.

COMFORT + FLARE = HIP-HOP WEAR

Before hip-hop dancers bust a move, they make sure they're sportin' the right hip-hop gear. When choosing hip-hop clothes, think comfort plus flare. Sweatpants, cargo pants, or loose-fitting jeans let you move easily in style. Tanks, T-shirts, sweatshirts, and jerseys are good choices for on top. And it's always a good idea to layer. That way when your body warms up, you can cool down by removing a layer.

On your feet? You can get started doing the fast footwork with your everyday pair of tennis shoes. But eventually you may want tennis shoes to wear just for dancing. Finally, finish your look with a hat or bandana.

8

Hip-hop clothing styles change quickly. Different parts of the country have different hip-hop styles. Find a style that works for you, but be ready to try new things. No matter what style you choose, remember that comfort is key. That way you can concentrate on your moves.

Choosing music

Combine cool moves and stylin' clothes with fast-moving music. You can even buy instrumental versions of many hip-hop hits.

Chapter Three

MOVING WITH STYLE

GOOD HIP-HOP DANCERS MAKE DOING THE MOVES LOOK EASY.

But becoming good takes a lot of patience and practice. Before you start, get a feel for hip-hop's attitude and artistic style by watching dancers. Check out a hip-hop dance DVD or watch a local hip-hop competition.

To be the best on the block, you might need a little one-on-one help.

Taking a hip-hop dance class will help you learn the moves. Or maybe someone at school with killer hip-hop moves can teach you. And of course, try some of the basic moves on the upcoming pages. Don't worry if these moves feel awkward at first. Soon you'll master the moves and be able to do them with your own style.

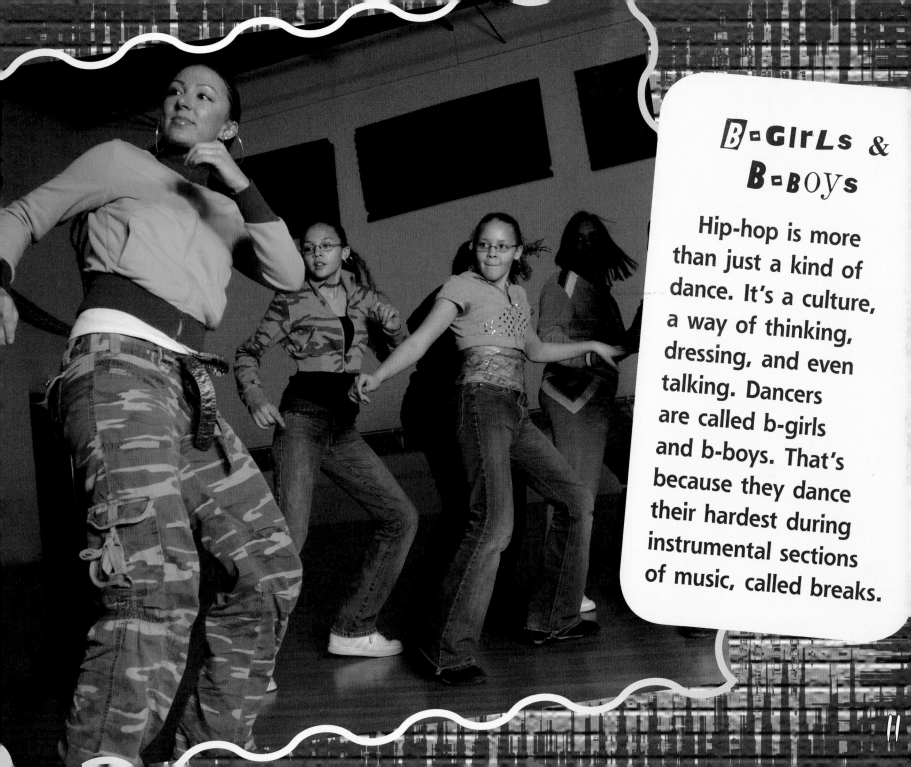

B-GIrLs & B-BOys

Hip-hop is more than just a kind of dance. It's a culture, a way of thinking, dressing, and even talking. Dancers are called b-girls and b-boys. That's because they dance their hardest during instrumental sections of music, called breaks.

POPPING

Popping is all about isolating parts of your body. Dancers pop by quickly tensing the muscles in a certain area and then relaxing them. Dancers often pop their head, arms, and legs. A California dancer named Boogaloo Sam created this style with his group the Electric Boogaloos in the 1970s.

THE FRESNO

To do a popping move called the Fresno, bend down and put your right arm out in front of your left knee. Flex or pop your arm muscles at the elbow to the beat of the music. Then relax your muscles and lean your body to the right. Try the same move with your left arm. Keep switching arms until the song is over. You can do the same popping moves with your legs, just above the knees. Once you get comfortable, try adding your own flare to the move.

LOCKING

No matter how loose they get, dancers include pause or freeze-type movements. This dance style is called locking. It was invented in the early 1970s by California dancer Don Campbell. When dancers lock, it looks like they're pointing places. That's because they are! Lockers also may make silly, clown-like faces to keep it funky.

"EVERY SONG HAS A FEELING. LEARN HOW TO GET INTO THEM. REMEMBER, IT IS NOT ABOUT MOVES; IT'S ABOUT DANCING. LOOK FOR YOUR OWN FLAVOR. THIS DANCE IS ABOUT THE INDIVIDUAL."
—DON CAMPBELL, LOCKING PIONEER

BASIC LOCK STEP

When you do the basic lock step, pretend you have a heavy, wet towel in each hand. Start with your hands at your sides. First, throw the towels up, making a squared off "Y" with your arms. Next, bring your arms back down to your sides. Finally, lock by pulling your elbows up and forward as if you're resting them on a table. If you do it right, it'll look like your joints are locking and you can't move.

BASIC TOPROCK

Before you bend down and quickly move from one breaking move to the next, you'll need a move that gains interest and respect. Time to show some attitude!

The fancy footwork of the toprock lets you play with the beat of the music and show your style. Start by putting your hands on your hips and pointing your right foot out in front of you. Next, put your legs in jumping jack position and cross your wrists in front of you. Finish rocking by placing your hands on your hips and pointing your left leg out. Now make the move your own by adding some attitude to the arm movements.

BREAKING

Here's the breakdown on breaking. Breaking started in the South Bronx neighborhoods of New York City in the 1970s. Street dancers competed to outdo each other with headspins, backspins, original moves, and attitude. Today, early moves such as headspins and backspins are still done. And breakers continue to invent new moves.

SAY WhAt?

You may have also heard breaking called breakdancing. As the dance got popular, the media started calling it breakdancing. But most breakers still call it breaking.

3-STEP

Most of the crowd-pleasing breaking moves you've seen probably took place on the floor. Ready to get down?

Start simple with the 3-step. Begin in a reverse push-up position, with your stomach facing the ceiling. Bend both legs under you. Kick out your right leg. Then bend your right leg and kick your left leg out. Twist your body to the right and you'll end up in a push-up position. Turn back to the reverse push-up position and keep steppin'. This move will take some crazy coordination, but you will master it in no time.

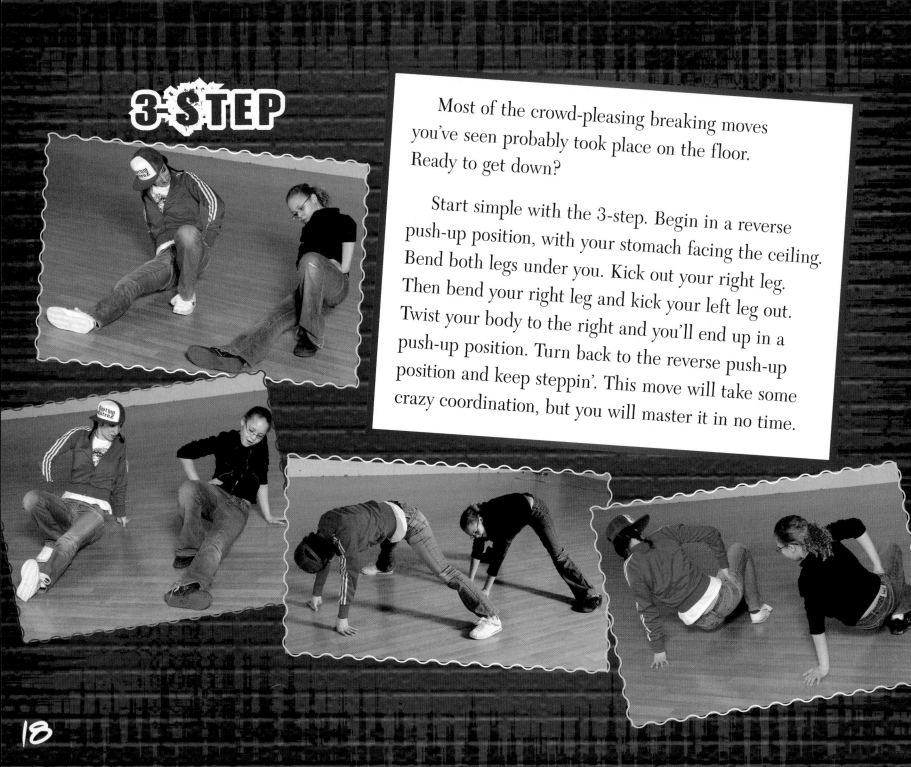

BACKSPIN

This breaking move will get you spinning, hip-hop style. Start by sitting on the ground with your right leg bent. Put your hands flat on the floor behind your back. Twist your body to the left.

Quickly kick your right leg to the right. Then kick your left leg behind your right leg. Keep rotating which leg kicks. Speed up your spin by folding your legs in toward your chest.

THE CRADLE

Want to end your breaking routine in style? Wow people by finishing with a breaking move called a freeze. Try a mini-handstand called the cradle. Start this move by sitting with your feet tucked under your bottom and your knees spread apart. Press your arms together, lining them up from the elbows to the wrists. Position your elbows in your belly button and place your hands on the floor. Lift yourself up onto your hands and freeze. Be sure to turn your head to the side, so that you don't bonk your nose if you accidentally fall.

"THIS DANCE (BREAKING) WAS BORN HERE, RIGHT HERE IN THE SOUTH BRONX, AND HOW MANY OTHER DANCES HAVE BEEN CREATED OVER THE PAST 25 YEARS THAT HAVE SURVIVED THIS LONG? IT'S A TRUE AMERICAN ART FORM."

—RICHIE COLON "CRAZY LEGS," LEGENDARY B-BOY AND MEMBER OF THE ROCK STEADY CREW

PUTTING IT TOGETHER

NOW THAT YOU KNOW SOME MOVES, START PRACTICING.

When you feel confident doing one move, try a different move right after it. You can put a set of moves together to make a combination. Working in small sections makes it easier to dance to a full song.

You and your friends can create your own hip-hop dances. But don't forget to add one of the most important hip-hop elements to your combination—freestyling.

23

FREESTYLING

Freestyling means performing without a set plan. Hip-hop dancers, DJs, MCs, and graffiti artists all freestyle. It's their chance to be creative and express themselves.

Here's a good way for you and your friends to practice freestyle hip-hop dancing. Stand in a circle with the music on. One person takes a turn dancing in the middle of the circle, called a cypher. After a short while, another person takes a turn dancing in the middle. Dance until everyone has had a chance to freestyle or until you're all exhausted!

BATTLE MANIA

Freestyling will get you used to showing off your moves. When your moves are clean and original you'll be ready for the next step—competitions.

Hip-hop competitions, better known as battles, take place at performing arts centers, in dance clubs, and sometimes even on the street. Dancers battle by taking turns showing off their best moves alone or with a crew. Large, formal battles are planned, but many small battles take place with almost no notice. Unplanned battles are informal, with the crowd watching the dancers to decide who the winner is. The winner gets the ultimate prize—respect!

SHOW 'EM WHAT YOU GOT

Dancers who want more than just respect sign up to compete in formal battles. At these battles, the top three crews usually receive medals and cash.

The crews, made up of five to eight dancers, have only two minutes to impress the judges. The judges award points to the crews. The crew with the highest score wins. So what are the judges looking for?

Judges give high points to moves that are original, full of personality, and smooth with few mistakes. They also look for dancers who freestyle with ease and grace. A perfect performance will earn a crew 10 points.